THE CULTURAL GAFFES POCKETBOOK

By Angelena Boden   *Drawings by Ph*

"As we move into the 21st Century customers will be looking to
to offer exceptional service standards. This excellent little book
visitors from overseas to achieve a higher level of understandin
Pat Powell, Personnel Manager, Cadbury World

"One of the joys of contemporary life which Britons are discovering through tourism and travel is the variety of lifestyles which can be experienced throughout the modern world. Britain, over the years, has acquired a reputation as a country that does things its way and, if the overseas visitor understands and adapts, so much the better. But sometimes it is quite hard to find out how to behave and, after all, should the adjustment be all one way? Life in Britain is changing very fast and, as our island community becomes more international, we are recognising how much more flexibility we have to demonstrate to our visitors.

The British Tourist Authority has the task of attracting visitors from all over the world (24 million in 1996); the quality of the British welcome will be crucial to making their stay enjoyable and making it more likely that the visitor will wish to come again. We are very fortunate that someone with the experience of Angelena Boden is the Master Trainer for Welcome Host International, the BTA programme set up to help those greeting visitors on their arrival in Britain. This pocketbook is a vital aid to all those engaged in the business. Our prosperity depends to a large extent on the health of inbound tourism."
Anthony Sell, Chief Executive, British Tourist Authority

CONTENTS

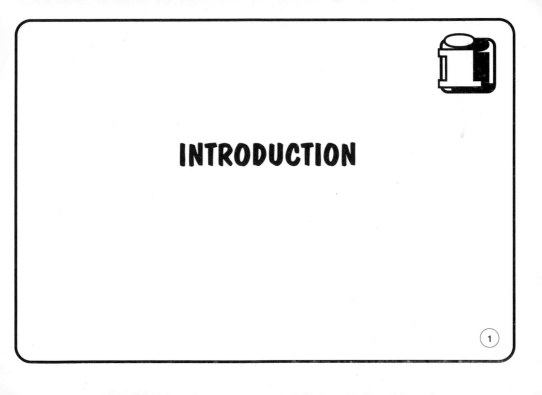

INTRODUCTION

AUTHOR'S NOTE

The Cultural Gaffes Pocketbook draws on experiences of people in their dealings with a range of overseas visitors, on national characteristics as outlined by tourist authorities around the world and, occasionally, on the people themselves.

The Author wishes to acknowledge the British Tourist Authority and other Tourist Boards for their help, advice and information.

It is important to remember that, while generalisations can be drawn when dealing with different nationalities, people are individuals and will not necessarily fit the general image. Regional differences, social background and education have an impact on how we behave and these need to be taken into account.

The British might be described as cold, reserved, lazy and snobbish, but that doesn't apply to me; does it you?

WHO SHOULD READ THIS BOOK?

This book is for anyone who meets and greets visitors from overseas:

● You may be working in the tourism and hospitality industry where you will be meeting visitors from all over the world

Or, alternatively

● You may be working as a receptionist for a large company involved in importing and exporting; company representatives from your trading partners may visit you from time to time

In both cases you will want to create an especially good impression and to show that you have some understanding of their needs.

REGIONS COVERED BY THIS BOOK

In this book we cover broadly the following areas:

- **North America** - United States and Canada

- **Western Europe** - specifically differences between Germans, French, Italians and Dutch

- **Britain** - national characteristics

- **Eastern Europe** - emerging economies of Czech Republic and Russia

- **Middle East** - concentrating on the Muslim and Jewish world

- **India** - Hindus and Sikhs

- **Far East** - Korea and Japan

WHY MAKE A SPECIAL EFFORT?

Business, whether it is manufacturing or tourism, is becoming more and more competitive. To keep ahead it is essential that companies give a consistently good service to all their customers, especially those from overseas.

People remember people. If you make your Japanese guests feel at home by greeting them in their own language or by being mindful of their dietary needs, they will remember you and consequently the company - they should want to do business with you again.

Companies can choose anywhere in the world to do business. Price and quality are only one factor; the attitude of the people they are dealing with is also very important. Misunderstandings occur when we British, for instance, misjudge other nationalities or make unfavourable comparisons with our own ways of doing things.

BENEFITS OF CULTURAL AWARENESS
FROM THE VISITOR'S VIEWPOINT

- Receives a positive first impression

- Feels more relaxed

- Senses a feeling of warmth

- Sees company as being enlightened

- Encouraged to do business again

- Likely to recommend company to others

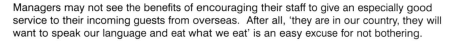

BENEFITS OF CULTURAL AWARENESS
FROM THE BUSINESS'S VIEWPOINT

Managers may not see the benefits of encouraging their staff to give an especially good service to their incoming guests from overseas. After all, 'they are in our country, they will want to speak our language and eat what we eat' is an easy excuse for not bothering.

Businesses that are culturally aware set themselves apart from their competitors by:

- Finding out about their foreign clients; their likes, dislikes and expectations

- Equipping their key staff, especially front line, with some greetings in the visitor's own language and some ground rules for looking after them

- Avoiding giving offence to their visitors through ignorance or assumptions

BENEFITS OF CULTURAL AWARENESS

FROM THE EMPLOYEE'S VIEWPOINT

- Experiences a sense of achievement and satisfaction when thanked or complimented

- Widens understanding of other people

- Progresses career through personal development

WHAT DO YOU NEED TO KNOW?

It is impossible to cover everything relating to the needs of visitors from all over the world. Some of the key areas will be covered in this book:

- **Courtesies** - how to meet and greet your visitors, including appropriate body language, degrees of formality and suitable topics of conversation

- **Food** - likes, dislikes and restrictions

- **Accommodation** - preferences and needs

- **Entertainment and relaxation** - what the different nationalities expect or look forward to and what would be most unsuitable

- **Business formalities** - present giving, direct or indirect approaches, appropriate levels of detail

STEREOTYPING

When we stereotype a nation and its people, what do we do? We:

- Put them into categories
- Attach labels
- Become subjective
- Reinforce our own prejudices
- Forget about the individual differences

Why is it damaging? Because:

- We don't give people a chance to prove wrong the stereotype
- It can lead to prejudice and strained relationships
- Barriers go up subconsciously and this affects attitude
- Such images spread quickly and become distorted

NORTH AMERICA

VISITORS FROM NORTH AMERICA

Subtle cultural differences exist between Americans and Canadians. In addition, attitudes and expectations vary between the states and provinces.

Canadians can become very prickly if you assume they are from the United States. Avoid the classic mistake: 'Which part of the US are you from?' The reply might be: 'Unless there's been volcanic activity that I don't know about, Vancouver isn't in the States.'

Canadians have a dry sense of humour and are considered quieter than their American neighbours. Apart from the North American Indians, their racial roots are in Britain, France and elsewhere in Europe.

The Canadian accent is softer, their manner less forthright and even the language differs. The word 'neat' is used a lot to show approval.

NORTH AMERICA

GREETINGS & COURTESIES

North Americans in general are renowned for their openness, warmth and hospitality.

- Make your greeting animated
- A friendly, firm handshake with good eye contact is essential
- Use their name as soon as you know it
- Small talk is important (especially if it relates to their trip) but avoid politics and religion
- Positive responses, said with an enthusiastic tone of voice, keep them buzzing, eg: 'No problem, I'll do that right away!'

French-Canadians will be more demonstrative - a kiss on both cheeks if you have met before.

DIFFERENCES IN COMMUNICATION

The North American accent is infectious. It is easy to find yourself copying it. Unless you have learned English from Americans, just be yourself.

- Try to understand them without questioning or commenting on the different words and expressions; 'Oh, you mean toilet? Ah!' doesn't go down very well
- Avoid unnatural speech
- Don't overpronounce - they tend to be self-conscious about their use of English
- Talk honestly and directly
- Use positive, helpful language

Note *Americans often make statements instead of asking questions. They are not always waiting for a reply, as with: 'So this is England!'.*

NORTH AMERICA

BODY LANGUAGE

- Dismissive gestures, eg: walking away, rolling eyes heavenwards, are particularly irritating to Americans

- Smiling into the eyes is so important; be genuine

- Avoid touching people

- Don't get too close;
  give them space

- Be animated

FOOD & DRINK

Americans enjoy low cost, fresh food in amazing varieties. Ethnic influences - Mexican, Chinese and Italian - are popular. Sumptuous quantities are offered. The tendency is to use only a fork.

Criticisms of food service made by North Americans when abroad can include:

- Food is bland
- No free coffee refills
- Portions too small
- Not enough choice
- No iced water on the tables

The golden rule? Choose restaurants carefully.
Check them out and speak to the manager.

Note *Americans like to do business whilst eating.*

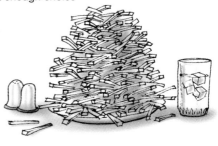

NORTH AMERICA

ACCOMMODATION

- Bed and breakfast is becoming very popular; a cosy environment, home cooking and a family atmosphere are most welcome; en-suite bathrooms, especially with shavers, are essential

- Little extras which become hidden costs are irritating to Americans; explain clearly what is included in the price

- Hotel bedrooms are often compared unfavourably to those 'back home' (smaller and more spartan); be prepared for possible comment

- First floor in the US is the ground floor in the UK

LEISURE & ENTERTAINMENT

WHERE TO TAKE THEM

- Anywhere where there is atmosphere which is typical of the area and which is of historic interest

- Quality restaurants which are a bit unusual (olde worlde places seem to be favourite) but check them out first

- Smoke-free areas; in Canada especially, smoking is banned in most public places

- Where service is friendly and efficient and quantities generous

If you're not sure, then take your guests to one of the chains they know.

 North Americans are used to tipping, as opposed to paying a service charge. Don't let them pay double unless they want to!

DOING BUSINESS

- It is common to exchange business cards
- Meetings are arranged by appointment
- Punctuality is essential
- Breaking appointments is considered rude
- Business dress required but many Americans 'dress down on Fridays'; check in advance!
- Smoking should be avoided
- Generous hospitality should be offered

It is unwise to leave Americans to 'do their own thing' unless they prefer that. Organising theatre tickets, dinner, guided tours, etc, is all part of hospitality.

FRIDAY
7.30 Breakfast (Guiseppe)
9.00 Production Meeting
10.00 Balloon Trip over Thames
12.00 Lunch (Wong's Restaurant)
1.30 Seminar
4.00 Bungee Jump
6.00 Gym
7.00 Theatre
10.00 Fish & Chips

19

SERVICE

Americans are used to a proactive service. This means offering before being asked.

- **Promote your services actively**, eg: in a hotel make it clear that the porters will carry the luggage to the room, a newspaper can be delivered and that guided walks, tickets, etc, can be arranged from reception

- **Check** to make sure the visitors have everything they need; offer complementary services, eg: point out that the swimming pool is often empty between 6.00 and 7.00 am

- **Be available**; Americans are used to a visible presence in hotels, restaurants, etc

- **Be detailed**; vague statements result in loss of confidence

USEFUL INFORMATION

- Writing the date: January 8th 1996 is written 1.8.96 (ie: month first)

- Driving: car rental companies need to point out rules of the road and offer a map; roundabouts, narrow roads, different speed restrictions cause problems; many American cars are automatic

- Special care should be taken when either selling or choosing clothes and shoes, as US, UK and European sizes differ (eg: in the US a woman's shoe size 6$\frac{1}{2}$ is a size 5 in the UK and a size 38 in Europe)

ARE YOU SURE THIS IS MY SIZE?

(21)

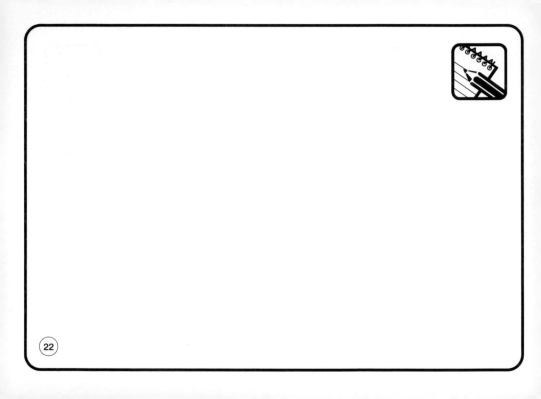

WESTERN EUROPE

DEFINING WESTERN EUROPE

It is easy to define Europeans as being all the same. While there are many similarities, this section will highlight some of the major differences in behaviour, attitude and expectations between some of the nationalities of Western Europe.

It is just as easy to offend German people as it is the Japanese!

While it is impractical to cover all countries, specific references will be made to France, Spain, The Netherlands, Germany, Italy, Switzerland and the Scandinavian countries.

GREETINGS & COURTESIES

- The biggest error we can make is to make assumptions about nationalities; 'The last time I was in Germany ...', when speaking to a native of Amsterdam, will be received with a cold stare, so find out where your visitors are from before you say anything!

- There is a distinct difference in the way the Germans and Dutch greet people compared with the Italians and Spaniards, ie: direct eye contact, firm handshakes, no-nonsense approach as opposed to warm smiles, kiss on both cheeks or pats on the shoulder, and oozing enthusiasm (Note: the French and Germans shake hands on arrival and departure)

- The French often insist on speaking French, the Irish use humour to break the ice, and the Scandinavians will put us to shame with impeccable English

Rule of thumb Follow their lead!

LANGUAGE

- People from Denmark, Norway, Sweden and The Netherlands speak excellent English; it is learnt in schools from an early age as it is a widely spoken language used in commerce and politics; however, they still appreciate a few words of welcome in their own language

- The French are proud of their language and prefer to speak it; the majority of French people will know some English but may be too shy to use it: relax them and give them confidence to use it by speaking some French; this will help to break down barriers

LANGUAGE

- For the Italians and Spaniards, it tends to be the younger people who know some English from school; try a greeting in their language and prepare to be bowled over by the response

- The city-based Germans will have good business English but it is a mistake to think that all are fluent; Austrians even less so

- The Swiss have three official languages - French, German and Italian

European visitors really do appreciate a few words of welcome in their own language. Try to acquire a few in several languages.

BODY LANGUAGE

- Some nationalities can be described as direct and forthright:
  - the Germans like direct eye contact and firm handshakes as do the Dutch
  - many use what might be considered abrupt and aggressive gestures - pointing, dismissive hand movements, 'posturing'; try to avoid mimicking or becoming defensive

- Others like the French are formal and may be seen as cold and aloof; stay warm and friendly without getting over-familiar - use Monsieur/Madame regularly

- Italians and Spaniards are tactile and like to hold on to the handshake, touch the arm, get physically close when talking; avoid backing off, they'll wonder what they've done wrong - Señor and Señora (Spanish), Signor and Signora (Italian) are always used

BODY LANGUAGE

- Scandinavians generally are friendly and open; they tend to respond to the way they are treated

- The Swiss like to shake hands when greeting and leaving; much use is made of formal titles

- A number of nationalities use the V-sign (offensive version) to indicate two or need for a cigarette, whereas the thumbs-up sign is not recommended for hitch-hiking (equivalent of the V-sign)

Note *When kissing on both cheeks, avoid making slurping noises! A light brush of the lips against the cheek is all that is required.*

(29)

WESTERN EUROPE

ATTITUDES

Attitudes vary throughout Europe towards family, culture, lifestyles, politics and life issues.

- Scandinavians are noted for being liberal in their attitudes; nudity, sex and the pursuit of leisure are not tangled up with guilt and hang-ups - be open minded!

- Spaniards and Italians, in particular, put their families at the centre of their lives; Italians will frequently telephone home to share their news

- The French have a joie de vivre to be envied; food, conversation, smart clothes and putting the world to rights are as important as work and money

- The Dutch like the outdoor life, are careful with money and have liberal views on euthanasia and smoking cannabis in public, while the Germans take an organisational approach to life in general

- **All are proud of their origins**

FOOD & DRINK

Choice of food is often influenced by climate and work patterns.

- People from the Mediterranean eat a healthy diet of salad, seafood, fish, vegetables and fruit; wine is cheap and is enjoyed with meals - Italian restaurants would be a safe choice; bread and iced water should be offered

- Germans and Dutch enjoy hearty food at lunchtime; rich desserts are particularly favoured, along with a good beer - choose a restaurant with a good choice, which seasons food well, serves plenty of bread and has first class service; because of the Indonesian influences, the Dutch are keen on exotic cuisine

- Scandinavians are noted for their smörgasbord, fish and a range of breads; alcohol is expensive in Scandinavia in an attempt to curb abuse, and wine is also expensive in Switzerland

- The French see themselves as the culinary masters; choose French restaurants or ones which have a French chef - it's easier on the nerves

ACCOMMODATION

It is difficult to make generalisations about the type of accommodation the European visitor prefers. International hotel chains do not pose a problem because of standardised rooms, facilities and services. There are some points worth noting:

- The Dutch and the Germans like bed and breakfast or youth hostels because of the cost and convenience; it's also a chance to mix with local people

- French hotels are graded on a star rating and bed and breakfast is only just becoming popular

- Germans, Swiss, Scandinavians and the Italians are used to a very high standard of cleanliness; value for money is more important than actual price

- Spaniards and Portuguese can offer cheap accommodation but of a good standard; similar types elsewhere might not compare

- Service is probably the most important factor; speedy, efficient, helpful and friendly service is sought - check this out first

LEISURE & ENTERTAINMENT

As with food, climate affects choice of recreational activity, but so does geography.

- The Dutch enjoy walking, climbing and cycling

- For the Portuguese, football is a national passion; the Spanish enjoy shopping, village life and mixing with local people - local craft fairs and markets are good places to take visitors

- Eating is a great pleasure for the French and Italians, but be prepared to linger over lunch or dinner for several hours

- The Germans have a rich history of their own and enjoy visiting heritage sites; they will have researched them well beforehand so you need to brush up your history! (The War is still a sensitive issue for many.)

- Scandinavians, in general, enjoy the sunshine and are keen to take advantage of it; bear this in mind when arranging meetings or trips to dungeons

DOING BUSINESS

IN GENERAL

- As with all Europeans, use titles: Monsieur/Madame, Señor/Señora, etc

- Business cards are exchanged frequently, dress is formal and appointments are made in advance

- Punctuality is considered common courtesy by most Europeans

- Smoking is widely accepted in France, Spain and Italy, although it may be banned by certain establishments; be tactful when asking your visitors not to smoke

DOING BUSINESS

SPECIFICALLY

- Meetings with the French tend to be formal and discussions lengthy, and they often entertain in restaurants rather than at home; it is considered impolite to begin a business discussion in French then have to revert to English (not so with tourists)

- Once you have made an appointment with a German, keep to it and be on time - punctuality is everything; appointments are often made by Germans earlier than in Britain; business is formal and a working knowledge of German is an advantage - be precise and stick to the point

- Italians and Spaniards are flexible about time - be relaxed about this

35

BRITAIN

VISITORS FROM BRITAIN

The British are a mixed race of Anglo Saxons, Celts and Normans, Gaelic, Cornish and Welsh and, more recently, Afro-Caribbeans, Asians and Chinese.

The dominant religion is Protestant and the government is an hereditary monarchy with Parliament having the real power.

Great Britain is an 'island' and it is often said that the people express an insular mentality.

English is the national language, but Welsh, Cornish, Gaelic and Manx are spoken in areas.

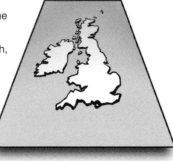

GREETINGS & COURTESIES

- Formal greetings are customary as is handshaking; the British are less demonstrative than many other nationalities and a reserved manner is expected

- If doing business, printed cards are exchanged as a matter of courtesy

- Neutral topics of opening conversation are more acceptable than exchanging personal information at a first meeting

- Religion and politics are best avoided

BODY LANGUAGE

- It is often difficult to tell what a British person is thinking

- The face is often unexpressive and not everyone smiles when you walk into a store or hotel; don't be put off by this but smile at them - it is just natural conservatism

- British people in general do not use hand gestures to emphasise points and can be critical of those who do

- There is initial eye contact but it tends to lessen as the conversation progresses; this improves if you help them to feel comfortable

- Avoid getting too close; the average Brit needs space (except in a queue - the British are well known for their habit of queuing)

BRITAIN

ATTITUDES

- Class divisions still exist in British society - people are often judged by the newspaper they read; private education is for the privileged or for those whose parents make major sacrifices

- British people are not as family orientated as other Europeans; children are still not welcomed in many places and couples prefer to find a babysitter rather than take children out with them

- Animals are much loved by many, with a large number of families owning a pet cat or dog; they may hold very strong views about countries which treat animals badly - avoid getting drawn in

- They are not noted for complaining if things go wrong; they will, however, moan when they get home and tell other people - so provide an opportunity for people to say how they feel and if anything is wrong

FOOD & DRINK

- It is untrue and unfair to say that British cooking is bland and unimaginative; many regional dishes are being rediscovered to replace the traditional fish and chips or Sunday roast

- British people enjoy their food providing it is well cooked, not too spicy and there's plenty of it

- Britain's multi-cultural cuisine encourages the people to become adventurous

- English breakfast is a treat for people on holidays as it is often the only time they indulge in bacon, eggs, tomatoes, mushrooms and fried bread

- Lunch tends to be a sandwich snack, with the evening meal the most important of the day; you may need to tempt them to try the local delicacy

FOOD & DRINK

- Tea is the national drink; hot, milky, in either a mug or a china cup - it is drunk at any time of the day

- Coffee is drunk but not as widely as in the rest of Europe

- For the English, beer and lager are widely drunk in pubs, restaurants and at home, while the Scots like their whisky

- A glass of sherry is a popular aperitif and wine is no longer restricted to a special occasion

44

EASTERN EUROPE

VISITORS FROM EASTERN EUROPE

Eastern Europe or Central Europe is sometimes known as the 'New Europe'. It is something of a mystery and source of curiosity. Countries such as Russia, Czech Republic, Bulgaria and Romania have opened up for tourism and trade and more people are travelling abroad.

Before looking at some specific cultural differences, it is important to note:

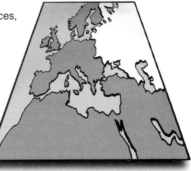

- Eastern Europeans do not want to be patronised: 'I bet you don't have this back in Moscow' will not go down well

- Many are prosperous, have travelled and are rapidly developing their economies; don't expect them to accept second class

GREETINGS & COURTESIES

- Many Eastern Europeans appear serious and formal at first meetings; Russians are often described as 'dour' but, in fact, are outgoing, warm and friendly people once you get to know them; Czechs, on the other hand, are conventionally friendly

- Handshaking is common when greeting and leaving; a full, sincere handshake (not the wet-lettuce type)

- Bear hugs become the norm with Russians and Bulgarians as you become friends; don't flinch, but return the embrace - it's a real sign of friendship

GREETINGS & COURTESIES

- Romanians greet friends with three kisses; men sometimes like to kiss women's hands

- Head nodding for agreement and shaking for denial are reversed in Bulgaria; you could have some fun with that!

Important Note *Many people from the former Communist countries treat strangers cautiously at first. Freedom of speech and movement is still a new experience after many years of repression and secret police.*

LANGUAGE

- As more Russian businessmen, students and the nouveau riche travel, English as an international language is becoming more widely understood; French and German are taught in schools; Russians use the Cyrillic alphabet

- Bulgarian is a Slavic language; Russian is Bulgaria's main second language with German and French widely spoken; it is mainly students who have a basic command of English

- For the Czechs, English is the first foreign language and the main business language; many Romanians are fluent in English

 Tip *Be prepared to speak French or German if your visitors don't speak much English. Always try a few words of welcome in their language.*

FOOD & DRINK

- Bread is an important part of any meal, especially black sour bread for the Russians

- Hearty, plain home-cooking using staple ingredients makes up the Central European diet; soups with beetroot (Russians), lentils (Bulgarians) and meatballs (Romanians) are national dishes, while Czechs eat a type of dumpling with meals

- Meat and chicken are often expensive, while fish, and in Russia, caviar, is cheap

- Many fruits have been imported, such as bananas, and these are a luxury; if your visitors want to buy fruit to take home, check that it is legal as foodstuffs are often disallowed through customs

FOOD & DRINK

- Czechs are famous for their beers; don't confuse German beers with theirs
- Main meals are often eaten at midday while dinner is a social occasion in the evening
- Hungarians do not usually talk during meals; goulash, their national dish, is a **soup** and not a stew
- Whatever you select, make sure the portions are substantial and the food is filling

Note *Fast food is still something of a novelty for many Eastern Europeans. Don't be afraid to suggest it!*

(51)

ACCOMMODATION

- In Russia and the Czech Republic there is a two-tier system of payment for hotels; foreigners often pay five times more than locals - your visitors need to know there is one system and price is based on quality and range of facilities

- Self-catering is a new concept to Bulgarians but private accommodation or home-stay programmes are common

- Accommodation has been state-run and of a much poorer standard than in the West; tourism is still in its infancy in most of these countries

Note *Select places which offer comfort, friendly attitude and good value as opposed to luxurious surroundings.*

LEISURE & ENTERTAINMENT

- Football, tennis and skiing will be of interest; Eastern Europe has produced some of the world's greatest sports people - it's worth checking up on some key names, past and present, in case the conversation turns to sport

- Folk festivals, dancing and crafts which reflect local life are popular entertainment; find out what's going on in your area that might interest your visitor

- Some of the finest museums and art galleries are to be found in the cities of Moscow, Sofia, Bucharest, etc; Prague is described as one of the most beautiful cities in Europe - don't think you have a monopoly on culture and architecture!

- Historic cities and scenic countryside will all appeal

EXPECTATIONS OF THE RICH COUNTRIES

They will be surprised to see:

- People sleeping rough, begging and other signs of poverty
- The amount and choice of food in the shops, and the range and number of cars on the road
- People having open discussions about politics, religion, etc, and discontent amongst people who seem to have everything
- Apparent lack of civic pride

Also, the 'plastic card' culture is alien to the majority who are not used to the idea of saving or having bank accounts.

DOING BUSINESS

There is little difference between Eastern Europeans and other Europeans when it comes to doing business; normal courtesies should be observed.

- Dress in a conservative but casual manner

- Expect long business lunches with the Czechs

- Punctuality, pre-arranged meetings well in advance and bilingual business cards are expected

- It is best to avoid July/August for meetings

- Be prepared for lengthy discussions and drawn-out bureaucracy

56

MIDDLE EAST

VISITORS FROM THE MIDDLE EAST

Think of the Middle East and probably the words terrorism, hostage and war come to mind. This can lead to a serious misconception about the people and their culture.

Arab nations - eg: Iraq, Saudi Arabia, Syria, Oman, Bahrain, Yemen, the United Arab Emirates and Palestine - are Muslim countries and the vast majority of people speak a form of Arabic.

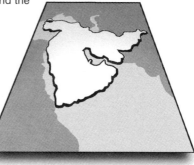

Israel is a Jewish country where people speak Hebrew.

Iran (formerly Persia) is a Muslim country but the people are **not** Arabs but mainly Persians. They speak Farsi. Turks, Baluchis and Kurds also make up the population and speak their own language. Iran has its own customs, many of which differ from those of Arab nations.

GREETINGS & COURTESIES

People from the Muslim world are hospitable but formal with strangers. Social and business etiquette is complex but here are a few tips to help:

- Avoid making direct eye contact for too long; men should not look directly at Arab and Iranian women - it is considered very offensive and could cause problems

- A standard Muslim greeting is 'Salaam Alaykom' which means 'Peace be upon you' - a Hebrew equivalent is 'Shalom'; it is greatly appreciated if you greet your visitors in this way

- It is essential that you observe Islamic politeness when addressing people - use titles and the full name; avoid becoming over-familiar

- Greetings are formal, often in a particular style and can be quite long-winded with lots of references to thanking God for good health, fortune and families

BODY LANGUAGE

- Eye contact is not as direct as in the West

- Avoid flirtatious gestures towards members of the opposite gender - eg: playing with hair, or other 'preening' gestures, singling out someone for special attention

- Whispering or holding private conversations when in a group are considered rude

- Too much arm waving or expressive hand gestures may give the impression that you want to be noticed; this would be frowned upon

BODY LANGUAGE

Pay particular attention to:

- The way you sit; showing the soles of your shoes, legs apart, and general slouching are offensive to Muslims

- Blowing your nose or cleaning your teeth with a toothpick should be done discreetly; turn your face away from your guests

- Blood is considered unclean; if you cut yourself, don't make an issue of it ('Oh gosh, look what I've done!') but excuse yourself to clean and bandage it

- **Not** admiring possessions; they will feel obliged to give items to you

ATTITUDES

There are some major differences in the way Muslims and non-Muslims conduct their daily lives.

- Some discussion topics (eg: married life, female family members, religious differences) are unacceptable and politics can be a very dangerous topic; talking about illness and death is commonplace (like talking about the weather!)

- Jews are less formal and are happy to talk about their country, religion and politics

- Hospitality customs dictate that if you arrive during mealtimes you are invited to join; bear this in mind if you plan to drop in at someone's house or hotel room

ATTITUDES

- There is much media attention paid to the Islamic dress code, especially in Iran; the general rule for men and women is to dress conservatively - skirts below the knee, high collars, long sleeves; women visiting Muslim countries should, however, check on current dress practices (especially regarding hair cover)

- Gambling is considered an evil by most Muslims; be careful who you encourage to have a flutter on the National Lottery

- Families are large and often include distant cousins; although not common, some Arab men of means do have more than one wife - avoid making remarks such as 'One for every day of the week then?' or 'You could take my wife off my hands', since he could take up the offer!

FOOD & DRINK

Sharing a meal is one of life's important pastimes, but there are some rules governing diet.

- Pork and pork products are forbidden by Islamic law; a pig roast carvery is not going to go down well!

- Halal meat comes from the ritual slaughter of animals for food (Jews call it kosher); it is inadvisable to discuss the rights or wrongs of this as many a westerner has been tempted to do; fish without scales (eg: shark and whale) are not eaten

  Caution: if rabbit is on the menu, then only legs and breast are acceptable

- Alcohol is also forbidden by Islamic law but there are vast numbers of men (rarely women) who drink beer and spirits once away from their homeland; it is best to avoid drinking in their presence unless invited to do so

- Never refuse hospitality unless you know them well

ACCOMMODATION

The spending power of Middle Eastern visitors will vary enormously from the incredible wealth of the Sheiks to average incomes of business people. Whatever their budget, bear several things in mind when organising accommodation:

- Muslims wash in running water - soapy water is considered dirty and so shower facilities should be available and offered (if someone asks for a private place to pray, ensure running water is available)

- A bidet is appreciated

- Newspapers in Arabic, Hebrew and Farsi show genuine consideration

- Discreet and formal service is preferable, so as not to draw attention to the individual

LEISURE & ENTERTAINMENT

It's unlikely that you will know how traditional or modern your visitors are in their outlook (this varies throughout the whole of the Islamic world), so it is a good idea to have several options available.

- Choose restaurants which serve halal food

- Vegetarian restaurants are safe bets

- Pubs are acceptable, especially ones with character and charm, although some may frown seeing children where alcohol is served; there should be something suitable on the menu

- If entertaining at home, include juices, fresh fruit, lard-free sweets and cakes, and chicken (even if not slaughtered ritually)

Note *If your guest burps after eating it is a sign of appreciation.*

DOING BUSINESS

- All business appointments are by prior arrangement; while you will be seen without an appointment, your dealings will amount to nothing; be prepared for an 11 o'clock meeting to begin around 12 o'clock

- Honesty is the only way to conduct business with Muslims

- Price negotiation is expected and enjoyed! However, a word of caution: once the price is fixed there's no going back

- Giving gifts is always done with the right hand; it is an insult to give with your left

- Doing business with Israelis is less formal but can be quite frustrating as you don't always get a direct answer to your question; don't organise anything on a Saturday, this is the Jewish Sabbath

Note *Some Arab men do not like doing business with women; be prepared for this.*

DEALING WITH MUSLIM WOMEN

Much depends on where the women come from, their family backgrounds, experiences of the western world, education and own attitudes as to how they behave. Some general guidelines:

- Mixed sports activities, especially swimming, may not be suitable

- Women are used to being together and not mixing with men socially; offering all-female activities will be helpful

- Many will observe some form of modest dress (not necessarily the veil); don't be surprised if they are covered on a very hot day

- Many women work, especially in the caring professions, but there are some, from Saudi Arabia especially, who live protected lives; if invited to someone's home for dinner it is very likely you will not see your hostess

THE FIVE PILLARS OF ISLAM

1. The profession of belief.

2. The Salah - five daily prayers. Some Muslims carry out all five prayers; others, because of work commitments, will restrict theirs to two.

3. Zakat - giving of money to the poor and needy.

4. Ramadam - a month-long fast from dawn to dusk. This includes water as well as food. It varies throughout the year. If expecting Muslim visitors, check whether or not it will be Ramadam as this may affect your schedules. You can't arrange a lunch meeting without everyone feeling uncomfortable.

5. Haj - the pilgrimage to Mecca.

JEWS

- The Holy Book is the Torah, the place of worship is the Synagogue and the religious leader the Rabbi

- The Sabbath is the holy day and begins before sundown on Friday and ends at nightfall on Saturday; during this period Jews cannot work, light fires, or turn on lights - candles are used to fill the house with light and the best silverware, cloths and dishes are used to celebrate

- Do not eat pork, rabbit, eels, frogs, shellfish or oil, milk or other products taken from non-kosher animals

- Kosher animals (permitted) include those which chew the cud and have a cloven hoof, eg: sheep, cattle, goat, deer and fish with fins and scales

- All kosher food has to be ritually slaughtered

- Meat and milk dishes should be separated and not eaten together; ice cream could not follow lamb casserole

- During Passover (7 days in spring) no food which contains yeast or dough that has risen can be eaten

JEWS

DRESS

- The Skull-cap is worn by men and boys in reverence and respect for God

- The six-pointed Star of David is a Jewish symbol

- Jews are not allowed to use wool and linen threads woven together in clothing (it is a forbidden mixture); avoid buying clothes as presents

71

INDIA

HINDUS

As well as being temporary visitors, many Hindus have made their permanent homes outside India. As with Muslims, their religion is intertwined with daily life, unlike in the West where the two are often separated.

Hinduism is a term for a religious tradition which takes into account both the history and social systems of India.

Hindus worship many gods and goddesses, believing that each one represents God. They believe in reincarnation and karma.

HINDUS

GREETINGS & COURTESIES

'Namaste' with hands together is the traditional greeting.

Although Hindi is one of many languages spoken in India, most Hindus speak excellent English and so language is not generally a barrier.

While men shake hands with men in western greeting, contact between men and women may be frowned upon.

INDIA

HINDUS
ATTITUDES

- Generally show interest in their different traditions and attitudes towards marriage, wedding ceremonies, family life, beliefs and keep an open mind - it can become an enriching experience

- One of the most difficult aspects of Hindu culture to understand is the caste system, which is based on inherited profession; inter-caste marriage is strictly forbidden so whatever your views on this, it is best to keep them to yourself

- Be aware of the sensitivity of India/Pakistan politics

- All guests, whether expected or not, are welcomed into the home and given something sweet to eat; try to be equally as hospitable to your Hindu visitors

HINDUS
FOOD & DRINK

- Indian food is based on a combination of flavours - hot and sour, hot and nutty, bitter and hot, sweet and salty; dishes are as varied as the regions of India and many have been taken to other countries by the new resident communities

- If you do eat out with your Indian guests, ask their advice on tastes and show interest in the food; this is very much appreciated

- Hindus have great respect for animals but the cow is particularly sacred; beef is therefore forbidden, so be careful when ordering food which might have beef content

- If you use your fingers for eating, use only the right hand and wash in the scented water brought to the table; food and utensils should not be touched with the left hand

- Hindus fast a lot, therefore it may be necessary to provide food and drink outside of normal serving hours

INDIA

SIKHS

Sikhs (a word meaning disciples) can be distinguished from Hindus by their outward appearance.

- The Gurdwara is the place of worship and the holy book is the Granth which contains the teachings of their Gurus; before entering any temple it is essential to remove shoes

- The three principles of being a Sikh are Work, Worship and Charity

- Sikhs speak Punjabi and, like anyone else, it is an important part of their identity; don't make the assumption that all Asians speak Indian - to show that you are knowledgeable will be a great compliment

SIKHS

APPEARANCE

- In most cases, the easiest way of distinguishing a Hindu from a Sikh male is by the turban; this is an outward symbol of their religion

- Sikh men (and women) are not supposed to cut their hair or shave; they are encouraged to maintain their natural appearance

- Sikh women wear the shalwar kameez (long tunic and trousers) and a dupatta - a long muslin scarf which they pull over their hair in the presence of male strangers or when going into the temple

- As with Hindus and Muslims, bathing in running water is very important, not only for hygienic reasons but it is part of Indian tradition; rooms with showers are essential

- Men are more likely to adopt western dress except for the tie which is seen as an unnecessary adornment

INDIA

SIKHS
CULTURE & CUSTOMS

- Sikhs don't smoke or drink, or eat ritually slaughtered (halal) meat

- Sikh men carry Singh (lion) after their name and women add Kaur (princess)

- Sikhs are not bound by the caste system

- Many are vegetarians

- Business is done very much along western lines with emphasis on hospitality and honest dealings

Note *If you are interested in some aspect of their culture, ask; they are nearly always willing to share experiences.*

BUDDHISM

It is certainly worth mentioning the millions of Buddhists in the eastern world, not only in India but also in China, Japan, Nepal, Malaysia and Thailand.

Buddhism is based on the teachings of the Buddha - the enlightened one who was a human being.

The main aspects of the religion can affect how we look after Buddhists:

- Don't kill or harm anything: this includes spiders, flies, wasps, etc

- Don't steal: this includes paperclips, time and using other people's phones without permission

- Don't misuse the senses: avoid having that last piece of gateau just to finish it up

- Don't use wrong speech: half truths, backbiting or gossip

- Avoid selfish behaviour: this is central to the Buddha's teaching

KOREA

KOREA

ABOUT THE COUNTRY

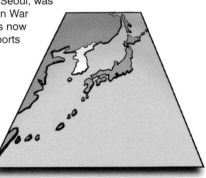

Korea is bordered on the North by Russia and China and to the East by Japan. Since the Second World War the country has been divided into North and South.

Fifty years ago South Korea, with its capital in Seoul, was mainly an agricultural country. After the Korean War (1950-3) it began to rebuild its economy and is now emerging as one of the Tiger Economies. Exports include textiles and cars, and more and more people are travelling abroad for holidays.

KOREA

GREETINGS & COURTESIES

While speakers of English use a number of vague expressions when meeting and greeting people they don't know (eg: 'Good morning, nice day, isn't it?') Koreans are much more definite in their approach.

- Don't be offended if a Korean asks: 'Where are you going?' 'What time are you going to eat?' 'What's that book you are reading?' Smile and just say something vague - that is what's expected!

- There is no need to keep saying thank you for things - it sounds insincere and vague to a Korean; try a more meaningful phrase, eg: after a meal you can say, 'I've eaten very well, it was lovely'

- Koreans consider it rude to be called by their first names unless you know them really well - in the workplace in Korea people are addressed by their titles; however, 'Mr', 'Mrs' and 'Miss' are acceptable by an English speaker

KOREA

BODY LANGUAGE

- Smiling in the West is considered a sign of warmth and being friendly; Koreans, however, view smiling at strangers as being too pushy - smiles are reserved for personal relationships, so don't overdo the flashing molars!

- Making a blunder will bring effusive apologies from certain nationalities such as the British; not so the Korean who will laugh out of embarrassment: it is a form of apology; don't get offended and think 'How rude!', but laugh along with them as this is like saying 'Don't worry about it!'

BODY LANGUAGE

- Casual hand gestures can cause misunderstandings; making a circle with your thumb and forefinger does not mean 'OK' - to the Korean it means money

- Finger to nose gestures are very rude, so it's best to keep your hands away from your face (even if your nose **is** itchy)

PARTICULAR COURTESIES

1. SAYING 'NO'

Saying 'no' when offered something is a sign of politeness. Say 'no' a couple of times, then **accept**. You don't have to eat/drink/smoke it. Refusal is what offends. Similarly, keep insisting if the position is reversed.

Avoid the following situation:

'Please have some cake.'
'No, thank you.'
'Sure?'
'No, thank you.'
'Ok, then. As you wish.'

Your Korean visitor will immediately conclude that your gesture was insincere. What does that tell him about you?

KOREA

PARTICULAR COURTESIES

2. INVITATIONS

- Whoever makes a suggestion to go out for a meal, drinks, to the cinema, etc **pays**; it is not acceptable to assume that everyone will pay their own way

- If your Korean visitor makes the suggestion and pays for the outing, take them somewhere else afterwards, for coffee or further drinks, so that you can pay; this will even it out and everyone feels comfortable

- At parties, Koreans will not expect to circulate as in the West but stay in small groups; don't leave your visitors to 'get on with it' - you can all circulate together

- Public displays of affection are an embarrassment to a Korean; men and women can appear to be quite cool with each other, whatever their relationship - don't try to change that

FOOD & DRINK

- Koreans are used to eating a number of small dishes at one time rather than in courses; they will eat according to personal preference and not in any order (as in Britain, ie: soup, fish, meat, desert, cheese, coffee)

- Rice is a main part of any meal and is eaten with a spoon; eat it neatly from the sides and avoid making a hole in the middle - this is a sign of poor manners

- Knives are strictly for the kitchen and cooking; don't offer knives - side dishes are eaten with chopsticks

- Koreans don't indulge in much conversation whilst eating; it is considered impolite - don't keep up a running commentary, instead savour the food

- Don't blow your nose whilst eating; this is a real turn-off

KOREA

FOOD & DRINK

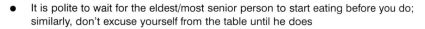

- It is polite to wait for the eldest/most senior person to start eating before you do; similarly, don't excuse yourself from the table until he does

- When eating from bowls, don't lift them to your mouth; leave them on the table

- **Never** stick your chopsticks or spoon straight up and down in your bowl (this is done at memorial services for the dead); instead, leave them on the table

- When holding out your glass/cup for a drink, hold it with your right hand and support it with your left; use both hands to pass a glass to someone - pour for others but not yourself; if in the company of someone very senior, turn your head away while you drink

- Avoid smoking

KOREA

LEISURE & ENTERTAINMENT

- Chinese, Japanese, Thai, and Korean restaurants or similar are very common throughout the world; find out what is close to you and visit it yourself

- Offer your visitor a choice; be able to say that you have eaten there yourself and the food and service were excellent

- Your Korean visitor might want to try local cooking; explain what is popular and how it is eaten - this avoids embarrassment later on

- Select somewhere traditional and not too noisy; the menu should be varied and should offer rice dishes, vegetables and salads - there is increasing interest in vegetarianism

- Explain local traditions and customs in restaurants during the meal; they will be looking to you for guidance

KOREA

USEFUL INFORMATION

- Koreans are unaware of the westerner's need for personal space; they tend to stand close to you when talking, brush past you, tug your sleeve to catch your attention and a number of other little gestures - no, they are not getting over-friendly; this is quite common and means nothing

- Koreans love children and will stroke their hair or clothing and hold their hands; don't panic

- Koreans have close-knit families and spend little time alone; if they ask you personal questions ('Are you married?', 'How old are you?', 'How much do you earn?'), bristling with indignation will not put them off; give vague answers if need be

- Knocking on doors to attract attention is a western custom; Koreans find it intrusive - cough or call out their name instead if you are providing room service

JAPAN

VISITORS FROM JAPAN

- Out of a population of 122 million, 77% of people live in cities

- Main religions practised are Shinto and Buddhism

- The Japanese are group-orientated and community-based people; this is an important consideration when looking after them in your country

- Japanese people travel on business, on honeymoon and as part of their wider education

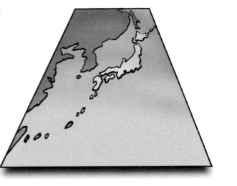

GREETINGS & COURTESIES

Japanese people are extremely polite and like to avoid confrontation at all costs.

- Avoid making too much direct eye contact; it can appear challenging and makes them feel uncomfortable

- Shake hands only when a Japanese person offers their hand; making physical contact of this kind remains an uncomfortable experience, especially for those not experienced in international travel

- While the Japanese do not expect you to bow, a sincere nod of the head is acceptable

- Be pleasant but reserved; dress conservatively

- Use titles and not first names

- Speak clearly, keep sentences short; try to neutralise any regional accent

LANGUAGE

While there has been an increasing number of people choosing to study Japanese instead of French and German, you don't need to know the language to appreciate the cultural reasons behind certain expressions.

'Yes' and 'No' are not as straightforward as they are in English:

- 'Hai' (yes) does not always mean yes, it can mean, 'Right, I see, I'm with you', or, simply, 'I'm listening'

- 'Iie' (no) is often avoided. The Japanese are reluctant to use direct language in order not to offend; you may have translated for you expressions such as 'We are keen to examine this further' - this would actually mean they are not really interested

LANGUAGE
HOW TO SAY 'NO'

- To convey 'no', the word '**difficult**' is used; don't try too hard to get round any difficulty in order to change their minds - when put in an uncomfortable situation the Japanese have a habit of sucking air through their teeth!

- Be aware of silences or gaps in the discussion and don't make the western mistake of trying to fill them; silence is after all 'golden'

- If speaking through an interpreter, avoid a two-way conversation; make some eye contact with every member of the group

FOOD & DRINK

- Fresh ingredients are most important, especially vegetables, fruit and fish; meat is not a traditional part of the diet

- Small portions in bowls are preferred for easy selection

- As a rule the Japanese dislike creamy sauces and strong smelling foods; cheese and dairy products are not generally eaten but, as with anywhere else in the world, the Japanese are acquiring a liking for the non-traditional

- Fruit is preferred to sugary desserts and green tea (ocha) is the best-loved drink in Japan

ACCOMMODATION

- Express checking in and out is helpful as is portering luggage to and from rooms

  - Twin beds are preferred; rooms offered to individuals in a group should be of the same standard

    - An unlucky room to be in is one with a 4 in the number; to the Japanese it means death

      - Regular showers followed by a soak in the bath are commonplace; some visitors don't realise that water doesn't drain away through an overflow and have been known to flood bathrooms

LEISURE & ENTERTAINMENT

- When taking Japanese visitors out to eat, choose somewhere that takes a pride in the presentation of food

- Japanese eat lunch at midday and do not usually linger more than one hour; it is a good idea to telephone the restaurant and arrange to be served immediately on arrival - see if you can organise a head waiter to look after your table

- Dinner is early in Japan (6.00 to 6.30); if you are meeting them at the restaurant, remember they are often early - be there in advance to welcome them

Note *If asked to take part in some activity, eg: song or magic tricks, do so willingly (even if you are curling up inside with embarrassment).*

JAPAN

LEISURE & ENTERTAINMENT

- Japan is a very sporty nation with an emphasis on health maintenance; baseball is the number one sport and pinball (pachinko) a national passion - arrange visits to fast-moving ball games which they are likely to understand

- Don't be surprised to see your Japanese visitors enjoying a quick game of space invaders; video games are very popular in Japan

- Choose attractions which are rich in heritage and are well known; if you can arrange a Japanese speaking guide, or at least leaflets in the language, this is always appreciated

- Craft demonstrations - pottery, knitting, painting, etc - appeal to women in particular, as Japan has many traditional fine art crafts

JAPAN

SERVICE ...

- Exceptionally high standards of service are required in hotels, shops, restaurants, etc

- If the Japanese need help they expect someone to be available immediately; check back with your guests in a non-obtrusive way to make sure they have everything they need

- Politeness, keeping your voice measured, patience and trying to see things from their point of view will be appreciated

- The Japanese will not complain directly but will wait until they return home - then they pull out all stops

... AND PAMPERING

The Japanese have refined pampering of customers to an art. Regular visits, telephone calls and gifts will encourage a friendly and more easy going relationship which will allow the occasional mistake.

Some ideas for pampering:

- Thank-you notes
- Newspaper clippings
- Seasonal gifts
- New brochure in Japanese
- Dinners and lunches
- Organised cinema, theatre, concert visits
- Quality gifts (beautifully presented)

This is if you wish to build a business relationship.

JAPAN

GIVING INFORMATION

The main point to remember is that lack of information will cause distress.

- Your Japanese visitor will have researched his trip in detail before coming; you can't fob him off with half truths or vague information

- Give as much information as possible; be precise and don't make assumptions, eg: if giving timetable details about a rail journey, include information about the number of stops, facilities on the train, platforms (if possible) and tell him not to worry if there are delays - it really does need to be this detailed

- Support materials such as maps, leaflets and sketches are really appreciated

RECEIVING & GIVING GIFTS

Giving gifts is an art in Japan and it is easy to offend. The following tips should help:

- If you are giving a gift (check that it is appropriate to do so first) it should be of good quality and possibly something made locally - glassware and pottery are sound ideas

- Gifts, like business cards, should be given with both hands accompanied by a few words

- Wrapping and presentation are important; Japanese like strong colours such as red and black - purple is not popular

- If you receive a gift, don't rip off the paper with a gleeful smile; ask before you unwrap it and avoid tearing the wrapping

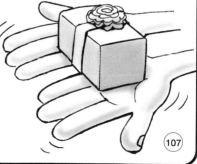

JAPAN

DOING BUSINESS

- Business cards are essential, preferably printed in Japanese on one side

- Offer and receive cards with both hands; your name should face the right way up to the recipient

- When offered a card, study it briefly before putting it away; avoid scribbling on it in front of the person

- When visiting your office, the Japanese will remove their coats before entering and will not put them on until their hosts are out of sight!

- There will be some protocol when making introductions, with the most senior taking the lead; it is important to establish a rapport with all members of the group and not just the ones who speak English

- Adopting a firm posture (avoid slouching) and minimising the hand waving to help make a point are advisable

About the Author

Angelena Boden, BA (Modern Languages) M.Soc.Sc. (Tourism) PGCE, is married to an Iranian-born computer software specialist and has two daughters, Anousheh and Anisa.

Angelena and her husband run a small business which specialises, amongst other things, in the development and delivery of training programmes for the tourism industry. She delivered language and cultural training in Atlanta in advance of the 1996 Olympic Games.

She is the Master Trainer and co-author for the English Tourist Board initiative, 'Welcome Host International', which is an introductory programme for staff meeting and greeting overseas visitors into Britain.

This edition published in 1997 by Management Pocketbooks Limited,
14 East Street, Alresford, Hampshire SO24 9EE

Printed in England by Alresford Press Limited, Alresford, Hampshire SO24 9QF

ISBN 1 870471 43 1

ORDER FORM

Your details

Name _____

Position _____

Company _____

Address _____

_____

_____

_____

Telephone _____

Facsimile _____

VAT No. (EC companies) _____

Your Order Ref _____

Please send me:

No. copies

The ___Cultural Gaffes___ Pocketbook ☐

The _____ Pocketbook ☐

The _____ Pocketbook ☐

The _____ Pocketbook ☐

The _____ Pocketbook ☐

The _____ Pocketbook ☐

The _____ Pocketbook ☐

MANAGEMENT POCKETBOOKS

**MANAGEMENT
POCKETBOOKS**
14 EAST STREET ALRESFORD
HAMPSHIRE SO24 9EE
Tel: (01962) 735573
Fax: (01962) 733637